YOUNG SCIENTIST

Volume 1

The planet Earth

World Book International

World Book, Inc.
a Scott Fetzer company
London Chicago Sydney Toronto

Illustrated by : Martin Bronkhurst
Jeremy Gower
Annabel Milne
Jeremy Pyke
Gwen Tourret
Pat Tourret
Matthew White

Acknowledgements

The publishers of **Young Scientist** acknowledge the following photographers, publishers, agencies and corporations for photographs used in this volume.

Cover	ESA (Science Photo Library)
6/7	ZEFA Picture Library
16/17	Spectrum Colour Library
18/19	Barr-Liaison (Frank Spooner Picture Library)
20/21	Novosti Press Agency (Science Photo Library)
28/29	Timothy O'Keefe (Bruce Coleman Ltd); Dallas and John Heaton (Spectrum Colour Library)
30/31	Doug Allan (Science Photo Library)
32/33	Spectrum Colour Library
40/41	J.H.C. Wilson (Robert Harding Picture Library)
44/45	ZEFA Picture Library
46/47	Nicholas Devore III (Bruce Coleman Ltd)
48/49	H. Bickel (ZEFA Picture Library)
50/51	Goebel (ZEFA Picture Library); Jan Taylor (Bruce Coleman Ltd); Ian Murphy (Tony Stone Worldwide)
52/53	Ron Rieke, Ung Werbestudio (ZEFA Picture Library)
54/55	Black Star (ZEFA Picture Library)
58/59	Sarah Ermington (Hutchison Library); R. Smith (ZEFA Picture Library)

Published by
World Book, Inc.
525 West Monroe Street
Chicago, IL 60661
U.S.A.

ISBN 0-7166-6353-8

Printed in the United States of America

7 8 9 10 99 98 97

Cover photograph
This picture of the Earth was taken by a weather satellite. The yellow areas show where clouds have formed in the atmosphere.

Contents

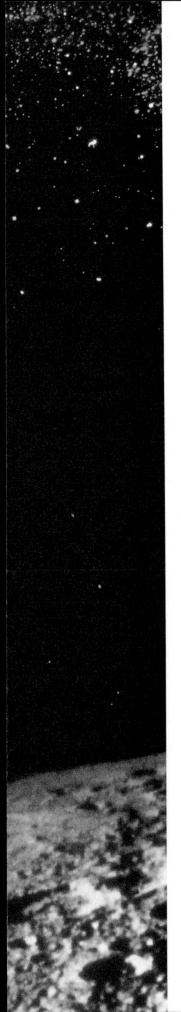

Our planet Earth

Imagine you are an astronaut travelling in a spaceship to the Moon! When you rise far above the surface of the Earth and look back at it, what do you think you would see? Astronauts who have been to the Moon say the Earth looks like a huge, blue ball shining in a black sky. The surface of the Earth is often covered with enormous patches of swirling, white cloud. The blue colour comes from the oceans of our planet. The black sky is the emptiness of outer space.

If you were an astronaut on the Moon, wouldn't you wonder how big the Earth really is? It would look quite small! But if you could dig your way straight to the middle of the Earth, your tunnel would be about 6,400 kilometres long.

Water, land and air

Our planet is one of nine planets that go around the Sun. All the planets receive energy from the Sun, but the Earth is the only planet which supports living things. This living world inhabits all the corners of the planet — its water, land and air.

Most of planet Earth's surface is covered by the blue seas and oceans. Only about one quarter of the surface is dry land. These landscapes are varied. They may be deserts, forests, grasslands, mountains or simply covered, like Antarctica, by ice. And all around the Earth there is the **atmosphere**. This is made up of several layers of air, containing mixtures of different gases.

This is the view of our planet Earth which astronauts would see from the Moon.

When the Earth was formed

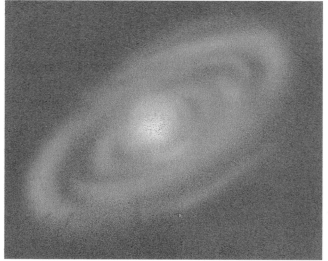

A cloud of gas and dust

How old is the Earth? No one really knows, but scientists think our planet is part of a **solar system** that began about 4,500 million years ago. In the darkness of space, a gigantic cloud of gas and dust once spun round like a huge flat wheel, millions and millions of kilometres across. This huge cloud is known as a **nebula**. Most of the gas in the nebula was hydrogen.

The beginning of the Sun

During thousands of millions of years, the nebula changed its shape. The spinning nebula pulled in gas and dust towards its centre. The force which pulls gas and dust together is called **gravity**.

The gravity of the spinning nebula pulled together a massive, tightly-packed lump, shaped like a ball. This was the beginning of the star we call the **Sun**.

Think of the time since the world began as being equal to the 12 months of the year. The first humans appeared at 5 p.m. on the last day of December.

Life on Earth

The Sun's heat and light provide energy throughout our solar system, but the Earth is the only planet on which we know there is life. Animals and plants survive on Earth because it is warm and has an atmosphere. The atmosphere provides air to breathe and protection from the Sun's harmful rays.

The solar system was formed

amoeba

| January | February | March | April | May | June |

The Sun shines brightly

As the new star grew larger and became more tightly packed, the gas at its centre became very hot, making the Sun shine brightly.

The solar system forms

Many scientists believe the Earth was formed about 4,500 million years ago. Far away from the shining Sun, the force of gravity began to pull gas and dust into much smaller centres, like whirlpools in space. Over millions of years, these also became tightly packed balls of gas and dust. Today, we know them as the nine planets of our solar system, all still spinning around the Sun.

Scientists believe that life on our planet began about 3,500 million years ago — that's only 1,000 million years after the Earth was formed. The first plants and animals lived in the oceans. Then, over 400 million years ago, living things appeared on dry land. Dinosaurs appeared 200 million years ago, and human beings didn't develop until 198 million years after that.

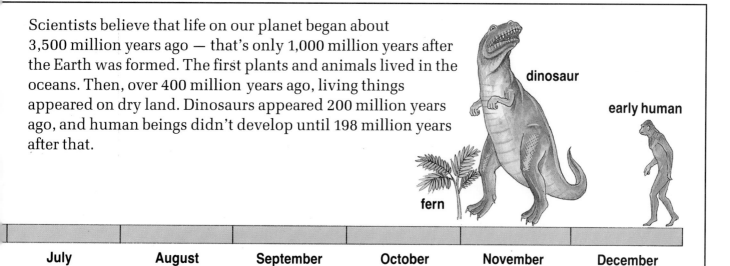

dinosaur

early human

fern

| July | August | September | October | November | December |

What is the Earth made of?

How do we know what is inside the Earth? Astronauts have travelled about 380,000 kilometres above the Earth's surface, but no one has ever been able to go very far beneath it.

The deepest mine that humans have ever dug is less than four kilometres deep, and the longest drill on an oil rig reaches less than eight kilometres. But the centre of our planet lies much deeper, about 6,400 kilometres below the surface of the Earth!

If you could cut a wedge out of the Earth, you would be able to see the different layers beneath the Earth's surface.

1,300 kilometres thick
7,000 degrees Celsius

2,250 kilometres thick
2,200 degrees Celsius

2,900 kilometres thick

32 kilometres thick

The **inner core** is the hottest part of the Earth. It is very heavy because most of it is made of iron and nickel.

The **outer core** is made of hot, liquid rocks containing iron, nickel and other metals.

The **mantle** contains mainly heavy rocks. In the deepest part of the mantle, these rocks melt because of very high temperatures.

The **crust** is like a hard, rocky shell around the Earth. It consists mostly of two types of rock — granite and basalt.

Inside the Earth

The outer layer of the Earth is called the **crust**. If the Earth were an apple, the crust would be its skin.

The crust that lies under the oceans is mostly made of a rock called **basalt.** It is about eight kilometres thick. The large areas of the Earth's crust which are not covered by oceans are mostly made of a rock called **granite**. These are the areas that we call land. They are the **continents** and **islands** of the planet.

The continental crust is usually about 32 kilometres thick. In some places, where there are high mountain ranges, it can be more than 40 kilometres thick. Underneath its crust, the Earth is made up of three layers of hot rocks and metals. These layers are called the **mantle**, the **outer core** and the **inner core**.

The layer of rock below the crust is the mantle. This mantle is 2,900 kilometres thick. At its deepest point, the mantle has a temperature as high as 2,200 degrees Celsius — hot enough to melt iron! Some of the rocks here are so hot that they are liquid, or molten. Under the mantle lies the outer core. This is made of molten rocks. The outer core has a temperature of about 2,200 degrees Celsius.

At the centre of the Earth

The centre of the Earth is called the inner core. Scientists believe that it is ball-shaped and made of iron and nickel. Here, the temperature is very high – about 7,000 degrees Celsius – but the metals are solid. This is because of the enormous pressure caused by all the other layers pressing down on top of them.

Find out more by looking at pages **36–37**

What is in the atmosphere?

Several layers of air surround our planet. Together, these are known as the **atmosphere**. The layer nearest to the Earth's surface is called the **troposphere**. It is about 10 kilometres thick at the poles and 16 kilometres thick at the Equator. About one-fifth of the troposphere is made up of oxygen. Nearly four-fifths is a gas called nitrogen, and the rest is made up of argon, carbon dioxide and small amounts of other gases. The top of the troposphere is called the **tropopause**. Here, the air does not have enough oxygen for living things to survive.

What is the ozone layer?

Above the tropopause lies the **stratosphere**. This layer is about 35 kilometres thick. It contains a gas called **ozone**, which is related to oxygen. The ozone acts as a protective shield around the Earth. Light from the Sun contains powerful ultraviolet rays which can be harmful to living things. Fortunately, the ozone layer stops most of these rays from reaching the Earth.

Air pressure

The layers of the atmosphere are rather like the blankets on a bed. If you lie under a lot of blankets, they feel heavy. The large mass of air in the atmosphere is very heavy and presses down hard on the Earth. Scientist call this **air pressure**. When you stand on the seashore, you are at sea-level. Here, more air presses down on you than anywhere else.

The farther up you go from the sea, the less dense the air becomes. Its pressure becomes less and less. In the top layer of the atmosphere, called the **ionosphere**, there is very little air pressure at all. About 1,600 kilometres above the Earth, the atmosphere fades into the airless emptiness of space.

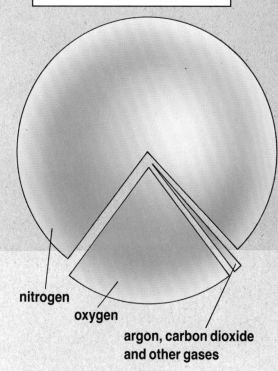

nitrogen

oxygen

argon, carbon dioxide and other gases

The troposphere is a mixture of gases. Nearly four-fifths is nitrogen. About one fifth is oxygen, and the rest is made up of argon, carbon dioxide and other gases.

This picture gives you some idea of what you might see in the main layers of the Earth's atmosphere.

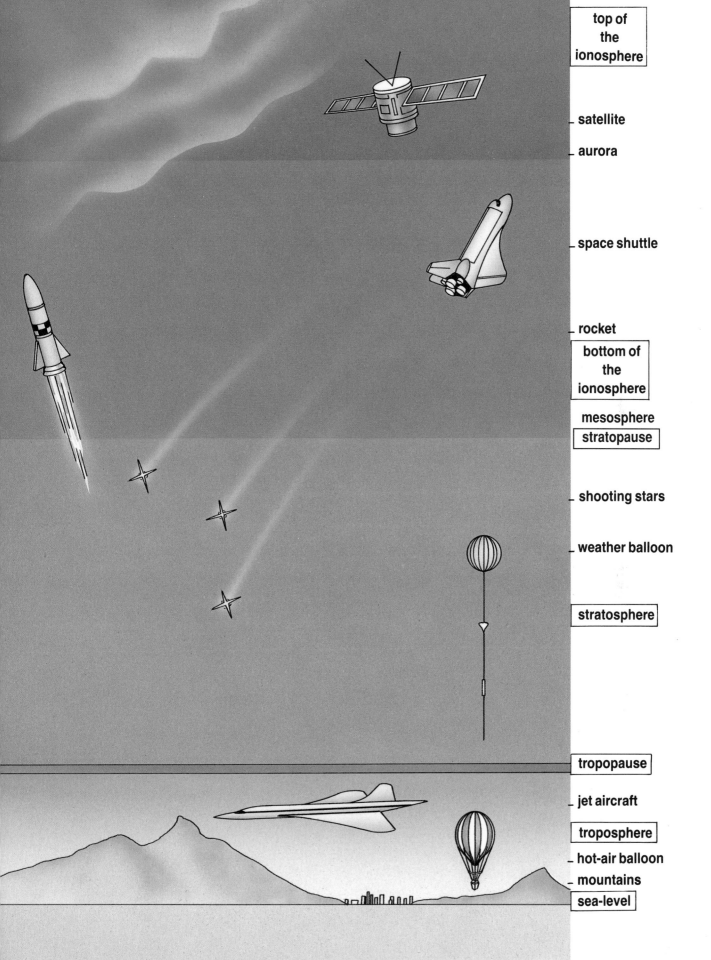

13

top of
the
ionosphere

satellite

aurora

space shuttle

rocket

bottom of
the
ionosphere

mesosphere

stratopause

shooting stars

weather balloon

stratosphere

tropopause

jet aircraft

troposphere

hot-air balloon

mountains

sea-level

Land on the move

Look at a map of the world. Can you see the shapes of Africa and South America? Does it look as if they will fit together? Make a jigsaw of the continents and find out if Africa and South America do fit together.

Moving continents

Early in the 20th century, a German scientist called Alfred Wegener studied fossils in the rocks from Africa and South America. He found the fossils were the remains of the same animals and plants.

He discovered that mountains in different countries might once have been joined together. The Cape Mountains in South Africa, for example, could have once been joined to mountains south of Buenos Aires, in Argentina.

Wegener believed that, over millions of years, the continents had gradually moved away from each other. They are still moving today. Scientists call this movement the **continental drift**.

All one land

You will need:

a map of the world

a pencil

a sheet of tracing paper

a piece of thin card

paper glue

scissors

1. Place the tracing paper over the map and trace the outlines of the continents.

2. Stick the tracing paper onto the thin card with glue. Cut out the shapes with scissors.

Pangaea

3. Now fit your jigsaw together. Do you think that the continents fit together well? Some scientists believe that the land masses of our planet once formed one huge continent, Pangaea.

Your jigsaw shapes won't fit together exactly, because the edges of the continents are under the sea.

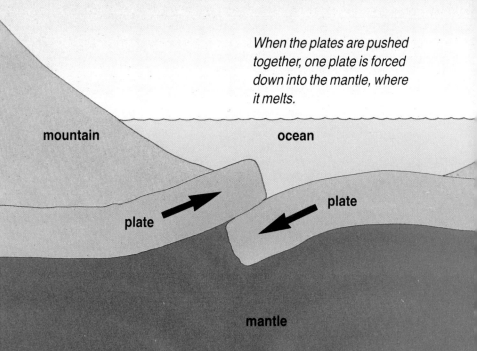

When the plates are pushed together, one plate is forced down into the mantle, where it melts.

mountain

ocean

plate

plate

mantle

Find out more by looking at
pages **10–11**
16–17

What are tectonic plates?

Many scientists now believe that the crust of the Earth is not formed in one huge piece, but is divided up into large sections, called **tectonic plates**. These solid plates are floating on the mantle, the layer of hot, liquid rocks moving underneath the Earth's crust.

What makes the plates move? It's so hot inside the Earth, that some of the molten rocks in the mantle are pushed upwards. These rocks break through the crust at the weakest points of the crust, usually where two plates meet. Then the plates are pushed apart.

In other places, cooler rocks in the mantle are pushed downwards towards the hot inner core. When the plates that make up the Earth's crust are pushed together, one plate is forced below the other and melts in the mantle.

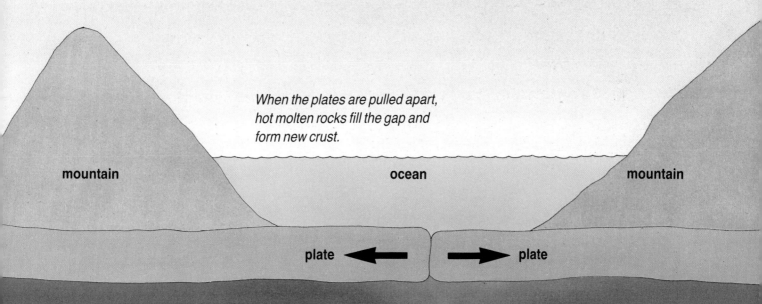

When the plates are pulled apart, hot molten rocks fill the gap and form new crust.

mountain

ocean

mountain

plate ← → plate

mantle

Find out more by looking at pages **14–15**

Making mountains

Can you believe that the top of the world's tallest mountain was once at the bottom of the sea? Scientists discovered this surprising fact when they examined **limestone** rocks from the top of Mount Everest, which is nearly nine kilometres above sea-level. Inside these rocks, they found the remains of dead sea creatures.

Limestone is a kind of rock that is formed in layers, very slowly over thousands of years. The skeletons of animals and the remains of plants that get trapped in one of these layers are changed into fossils. Scientists can tell when and where different creatures lived by examining fossils.

How did rocks from the bottom of the sea get to the top of our tallest mountain? More than 60 million years ago, India was pushed up against the continent of Asia. This happened because of movements in the huge plates of the Earth's crust. Before this, India and Asia were completely separate.

These rocks have been gradually pushed together to make a fold.

Mountains of the world

The mountains of the world have been formed in different ways. The Himalayas to the north of India, and the Alps to the north of Italy, were formed when plates in the Earth's crust were pushed together. When rocks buckle up, or fold in this way, we call them **fold mountains**.

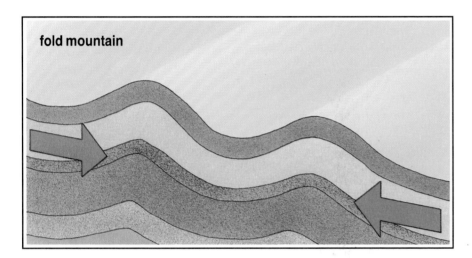

fold mountain

Another type of mountain is formed when movements of the plates inside the Earth's crust create weak areas, or **faults**, in the crust. As the plates press together, the mantle pushes its way upwards and cracks appear. The land between the cracks is forced up in a block-like shape. This type of mountain is called a **block mountain**. The Sierra Nevada in the USA and the mountain ranges of East Africa are examples of block mountains.

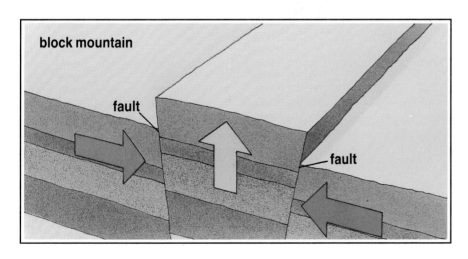

block mountain

fault

fault

A paper mountain range

Rocks feel hard and solid when you touch them. But when some rocks are pushed together with great force, they can bend and fold just like a pile of paper.

See for yourself how this can happen.

You will need:

a pile of paper, at least 5 mm thick

Think of each sheet of paper as a layer of rock.

What happens when you push the sheets of paper together? The sheets rise up into a peak. You have made a paper mountain range. In the same way, the Earth's movements have made mountains by pushing rocks together.

Find out more by looking at
pages **14–15**

*This map of the world shows that
volcanoes and earthquakes
usually occur in the same areas of
the world. These areas are
usually situated on the edges of the
tectonic plates.*

When the Earth shakes

Would you be frightened if the ground started shaking under
your feet? Sudden, violent movements under the Earth's
surface are called **earthquakes**. Sometimes, the ground
shakes so hard that buildings fall, roads and bridges are
smashed and electric power lines break.

Look at this map of the world. The thick, black lines show the
edges of the huge sections, or **tectonic plates**, in the Earth's
crust. The shaded areas show places where earthquakes are
strongest and happen most often. Most earthquakes occur
near the edges of the plates. Some of the earthquake areas,
or **zones**, are on the land, and some are under the sea.

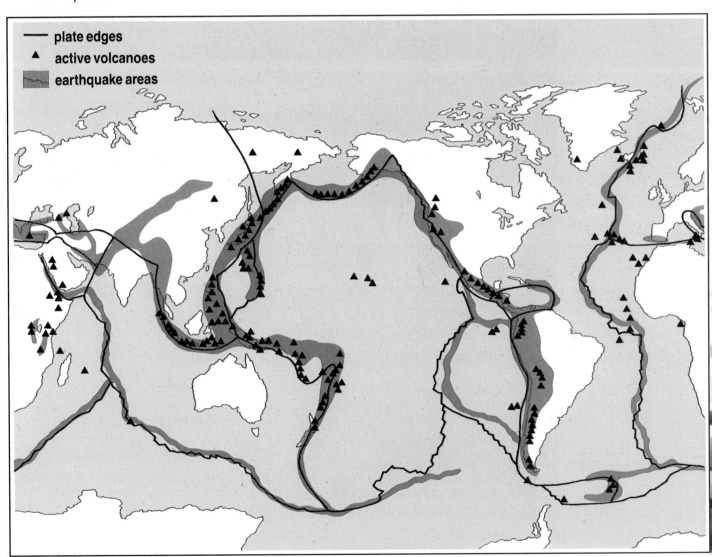

— plate edges
▲ active volcanoes
▨ earthquake areas

Earthquakes can cause widespread damage to homes, schools, factories and other buildings. This house was damaged during an earthquake in the USA.

Why do earthquakes happen?

At the edges of the plates, there are cracks, or **faults**, in the Earth's crust. Over many years, the plates slide past each other slowly, but sometimes the rocks get stuck together. Then the intense heat from inside the Earth goes on pushing at them until they bend. Eventually, the pressure suddenly jolts them free, sending shock waves through the ground.

Measuring earthquakes

Scientists measure the strength of an earthquake in two different ways. Using a measure called the **Richter Scale**, they measure the amount of energy that an earthquake releases and give it a score from 0 to 9. An earthquake that measures 9 is 100 million times stronger than one that measures 1.

The **Mercalli Scale** measures the amount of damage an earthquake causes, and gives the damage a score from 1 to 12. A score of 1 means no damage, but a score of 12 means the earthquake has destroyed whole buildings.

Giant waves

Earthquakes under the sea sometimes make giant ocean waves, called **tsunamis**. These destructive waves can be as high as 30 metres, and happen most often in the Pacific Ocean, near to Japan.

steam, gas and dust

When the Earth spits fire

Suddenly, a fountain of fire bursts out of the Earth, showering the land or sea with hot, liquid rock and clouds of dust and gas. This is what happens when a **volcano** erupts.

On our planet, there are about 530 active volcanoes, which might erupt at any time. Some of them lie under the sea. Each year, only about 25 volcanoes erupt. Some, such as Stromboli in Italy, erupt frequently.

On the map of the world on page 18, look at the edges of the large sections, or plates, in the Earth's crust. The shaded areas show where most earthquakes happen. Most volcanoes also occur near the edges of these plates.

volcanic bombs

flowing lava

layers of ash and lava

What happens inside the Earth?

Underneath its surface, the Earth is a mass of hot rocks and metals. In the mantle, the layer under the Earth's crust, it is so hot that the rocks have melted and become molten rocks.

As the rocks melt, they produce gases. The mixture of gas and molten rock is called **magma**. Because it is mixed with bubbles of gas, the molten rock weighs less than the solid rocks around it. The magma rises towards the Earth's surface and collects in hollow spaces called **chambers**. Some magma chambers are only three kilometres underground.

magma

A volcano erupts

Near the edges of the sections, or plates, there are weak places called cracks, or **fissures**. Strong pressure underground forces the magma to carve a tunnel up through these cracks. When the magma bursts out, a volcano erupts. Gases from the magma become part of the Earth's atmosphere, and a hot, fiery liquid, called **lava**, flows over the ground.

If the lava is quite thin, like soup, it spreads out and makes a wide, flat volcano. Mauna Loa, on Hawaii in the Pacific Ocean, is a volcano that was formed like this. When the lava is thick, like syrup, it makes a cone-shaped volcano with steep sides, such as Mount Fuji in Japan.

21

Find out more by looking at pages **10–11**
14–15
18–19

In 1988 a volcanic eruption on an island north of Japan produced a brilliant light show in the night sky.

Hot water and steam

Sometimes, gases in the magma leak out and heat up water in the rocks near the Earth's surface. Then jets of boiling water and steam, called **geysers**, burst out of the ground near a magma chamber.

How rocks are made

Take a close look at a small rock. Can you see tiny pieces of different colours and shapes in it? These pieces are called **minerals**. Most rocks are a mixture of different minerals. For example, **granite** consists mainly of quartz and two types of feldspar. It may also contain mica and hornblende.

Scientists who study rocks are called **geologist**s. Geologists have classified rocks and divided them into three main groups. The group a rock belongs to depends on how the rock was originally formed. These groups are **igneous** rock, **sedimentary** rock and **metamorphic** rock.

Igneous rocks

Molten rock that bursts from the mantle under the Earth's crust cools down and becomes solid. This is called igneous rock. You can clearly see crystal shapes in some igneous rocks, such as granite and basalt. Crystals are solids made from atoms arranged in an orderly pattern.

lava

magma

Sedimentary rocks

Small pieces of rock are washed down into the sea. These pieces settle in layers, or strata. Over millions of years, more and more layers press down on each other and turn the bottom layers into hard, sedimentary rock.

Sometimes, the remains of dead plants and animals turn to stone in the layers of sedimentary rocks. These remains, called fossils, tell us about life on Earth long ago when the rocks they were trapped in were formed.

You will need:

water

some dry, clean clay and sand

a tablespoon

a glass jar, with a lid

Shake and settle

1. Half fill the jar with water, and put in about four spoonfuls of clay and four spoonfuls of sand.

2. Screw the lid on tightly and shake the jar. Watch the clay and sand settle. The particles of sand are more dense so they settle first. Then the smaller, lighter clay particles make a layer on top.

Imagine this happening under the ocean for millions of years. Eventually, the weight of the top layers presses the lower layers into hard, sedimentary rock.

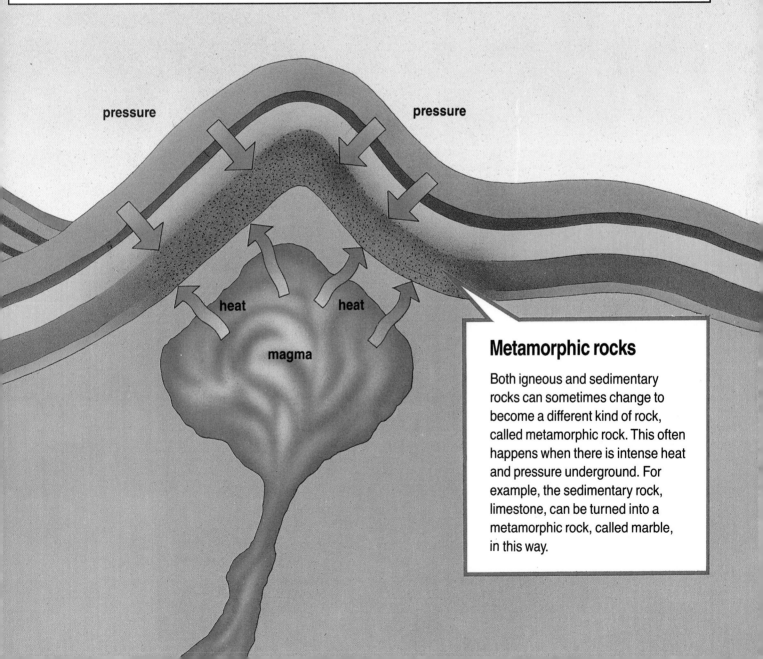

pressure

pressure

heat

heat

magma

Metamorphic rocks

Both igneous and sedimentary rocks can sometimes change to become a different kind of rock, called metamorphic rock. This often happens when there is intense heat and pressure underground. For example, the sedimentary rock, limestone, can be turned into a metamorphic rock, called marble, in this way.

Find out more by looking at pages **10–11**

What lies under the oceans?

Nearly three-quarters of the Earth's surface is covered by water. The land under the oceans is made up of mountains, valleys and large, flat plains, just like the land on the continents. It even has volcanoes!

The water in the sea

Where did the oceans come from? Some scientists believe that the oceans were formed about 4,000 million years ago. At this time, hot rocks inside the Earth cooled down and water vapour in the air fell as rain. The rain gradually filled the low places in the Earth's crust and formed the first oceans.

The **continental shelf** is the real edge of the continent, where the land slopes away to meet the sea-bed. It lies about 200 metres below sea-level.

Ocean ridges are found on the submarine plain. These are lines on the ocean floor where molten rock has pushed its way up from beneath the Earth's crust.

Away from the shelf, the sea-bed drops sharply to about 5,000 metres below sea-level. This area of flat sea-bed is called the **submarine plain**.

At the bottom of the sea

How do we know what lies at the bottom of the ocean? Scientists who study the ocean are called **oceanographers**. With the help of very accurate instruments, they have made maps of the ocean floor.

Modern oceanographers use a device called an **echo sounder** to measure the depth of an ocean. A transmitter on board an echo-sounding ship sends down sound waves to the ocean floor. A receiver helps scientists on board to measure how long it takes for the sound waves to echo back to the surface of the water. The longer the echoes take to return, the greater the depth.

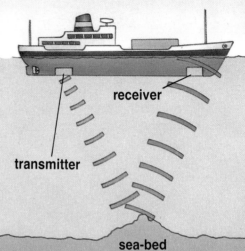

receiver

transmitter

sea-bed

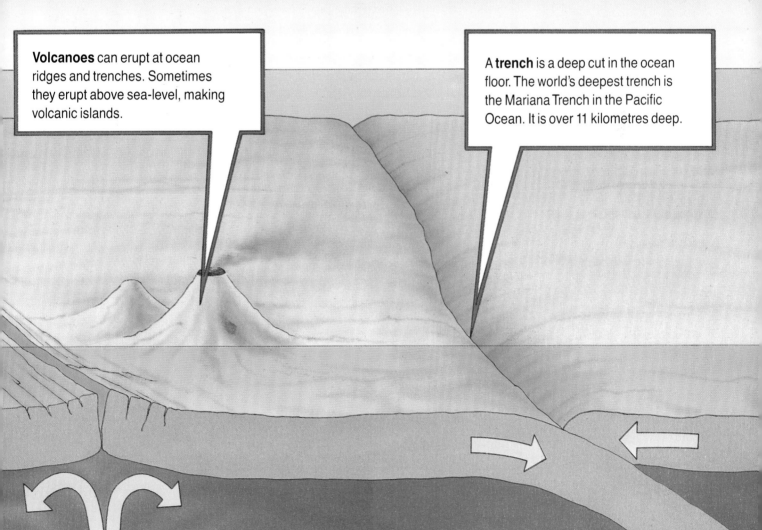

Volcanoes can erupt at ocean ridges and trenches. Sometimes they erupt above sea-level, making volcanic islands.

A **trench** is a deep cut in the ocean floor. The world's deepest trench is the Mariana Trench in the Pacific Ocean. It is over 11 kilometres deep.

Why does an ocean move?

The waters of an ocean are moving all the time. The surface of the water moves in **waves**, and the level of the ocean rises and falls with the **tides**. What makes these movements that we call waves and tides?

Waves are caused by winds which blow across the surface of the ocean. Waves themselves move forwards, but under each wave, the water moves around in a circle. As each wave reaches the shore, it breaks into surf.

Water on the surface of an ocean moves up and down while the waves travel along its surface. The water does not really move forwards until the wave reaches the shore.

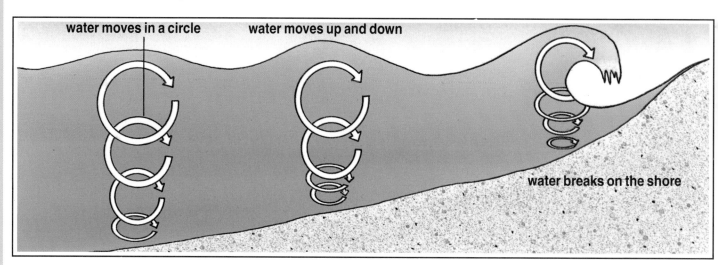

water moves in a circle   water moves up and down

water breaks on the shore

You will need:

a thin rope, 4 m long

a tree or post

Making waves

1. Tie one end of the rope to a tree or post, at the same height as your waist. Hold the other end and stand about three and a half metres away.

2. Move the rope quickly up and down. A wave moves along the rope, but the rope itself does not move forwards.

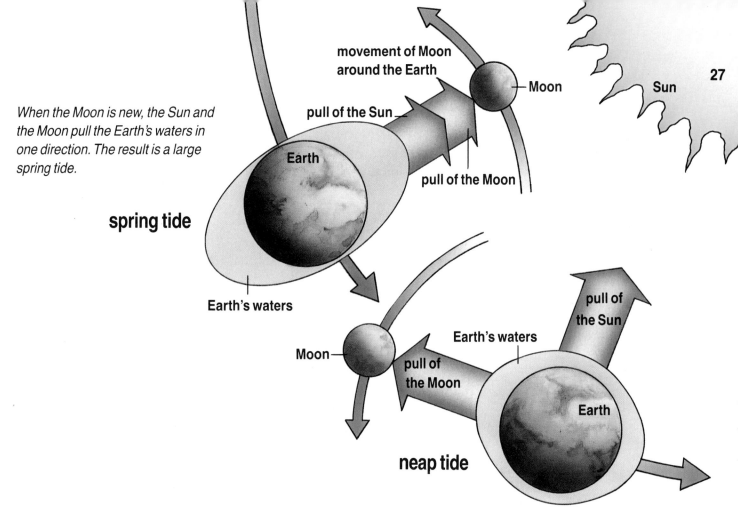

When the Moon is new, the Sun and the Moon pull the Earth's waters in one direction. The result is a large spring tide.

movement of Moon around the Earth

pull of the Sun

Moon

Sun

pull of the Moon

Earth

spring tide

Earth's waters

Moon

Earth's waters

pull of the Sun

pull of the Moon

Earth

neap tide

When the Moon is halfway between new and full, the pull of the Sun is at right angles to the pull of the Moon. The result is a small neap tide.

High tide and low tide

Have you ever gone to the beach to walk or play, but found it completely covered by water? Sometimes, you have to wait as long as six hours before the seashore is uncovered again! These changes in the level of water are called tides. **High tide** is when the water covers the shore. **Low tide** is when the beach is uncovered again.

Tides happen because of a force called **gravity**. The gravity of the Moon pulls the Earth's waters towards the Moon. And the gravity of the Sun pulls the Earth's waters towards the Sun.

The Moon takes about one month to move around the Earth. The direction in which the waters move depends on where the Moon is in the sky. When the Moon is either new or full, the Sun, Moon and Earth lie in a straight line. The tides that happen then are called **spring tides**. During spring tides, the difference between the level of water at high tide and at low tide is very large. When the Sun, Moon and Earth are at right angles to each other, the tides are called **neap tides**. This is when the difference between high tide and low tide is small.

The shape of the coast

The difference between the level of water at high tide and low tide also varies with the shape of the coast. On the coasts of the Mediterranean Sea, the difference may be as little as 30 centimetres. In the Bay of Fundy in eastern Canada, the difference may be as much as 12 metres.

Find out more by looking at
pages **22–23**
32–33

Wearing rocks away

Have you ever seen the waves pounding against the coastline? The force of the water moves the sand and pebbles on the beach. Sea and river water are always moving sand, soil and rocks from one place to another. This process is called **erosion**. Wind and ice also wear away, or erode, rocks and soil. Over thousands of years, erosion can move mountains, dig out or fill in valleys, and change the direction of rivers.

Rocks feel hard and solid. But they can be broken down. For example, water which seeps into cracks in rocks may freeze and become ice. The ice splits the rock and breaks it into smaller pieces. These pieces are washed away by seas and rivers, blown away by the wind, or moved down a mountain-side by a frozen river of ice called a **glacier**.

Over millions of years, loose stones carried along by large, fast-flowing rivers erode a passage through solid rock. The huge valleys they make are called **canyons**. In Arizona, in the United States of America, the Colorado River has carved a deep gorge called the Grand Canyon.

Chemicals in water can dissolve some rocks, leaving behind large caves. Rain water often mixes with carbon dioxide gas, making a weak acid that eats away some types of rock.

Parts of the Grand Canyon in Arizona, USA, are almost 30 km wide and 1½ km deep. The different layers of red and brown rock look especially brilliant at sunset.

In the Arches National Park in Utah, USA, the rock has been worn away to form two arches that have joined together.

How do rocks change?

Have you ever seen an archway of rock jutting out into the sea? The moving water has worn a hole through the weaker middle parts of this rock. You might see a rock arch inland, too. Strong winds blow sand against the rock, wearing away the weaker parts, but leaving the firm parts still in place.

Small pieces of rock that are washed or blown away form **sediment**. The sediment will settle somewhere in layers. Eventually, these layers are pressed together to make new rocks, called **sedimentary rocks**.

Flowing river water washes sand, clay and soil down towards the sea. In some places, where a river meets the sea, this sediment piles up in layers that form a piece of new land called a **delta**.

Icebreaker ships cut a path through the thick Antarctic ice, so that other ships can travel past.

When ice covers the Earth

Have you ever tried to make a snowball? Snow is soft and fluffy when it falls from the sky, but when you press it into a ball, it can become quite hard. If you press it very tightly, it turns into a lump of solid ice.

It is so cold at the North and South poles, that the snow there never has a chance to melt. As more snow falls, it presses down into tightly packed layers which then turn into ice.

Sheets of ice

Some areas of the Earth are covered by huge sheets of ice and snow all year round. Around the North Pole there is no land, but an **ice sheet** covers the Arctic Ocean. An ice sheet also covers most of Greenland and parts of Canada and Europe.

The largest ice sheet in the world lies around the South Pole. It covers about 14 million square kilometres of the huge continent called Antarctica. This ice sheet has an average thickness of 2,200 metres. The Antarctic ice contains about three-quarters of all the Earth's fresh water.

Our frozen past

For hundreds of years, many layers of ice have been forming in the Arctic and in Antarctica. Scientists can dig down into the ice to find traces of the past. They may find frozen grains of pollen that tell them what kinds of flower once grew on the surface of the planet.

Ice taken from deep down under the surface of Greenland shows that the air has been polluted with lead for hundreds of years. Samples of ice also prove that lead pollution has become much worse during the past 100 years. Scientists believe that most of this pollution is caused by the lead in petrol.

What is an Ice Age?

The huge ice sheets around the North and South poles were once even bigger than they are now! In the past, there were long periods of time when ice actually covered large areas of North America and northern Europe. These periods of time are called **Ice Ages**.

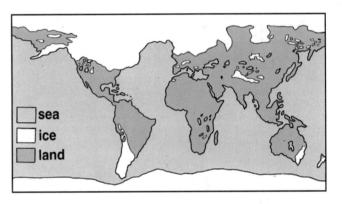

This map shows which areas of the world were covered with ice during the Pleistocene Ice Age.

The most recent Ice Age began about 2 million years ago, and is known as the Pleistocene Ice Age. During each Ice Age, the ice advances and retreats several times.

In past Ice Ages, each advance of ice, or **glaciation**, lasted about 100,000 years. In between glaciations there were **interglacial periods** of about 10,000 years, when the ice melted and retreated.

Why do Ice Ages happen?

Most scientists believe that Ice Ages are caused by a regular change in the way the Earth moves around the Sun.
This change seems to happen every 100,000 years, when the surface of the planet cools and huge ice sheets form.
If this is true, we are now living in an interglacial period.
And some time in the future, the ice will advance again!

Glaciers and icebergs

In mountainous regions, a river of ice may flow down a valley. This is called a **glacier**. A glacier can move at different speeds, from a few centimetres every year to as much as 200 metres every year.

How a glacier begins

Glaciers begin as small dips or hollows on the mountainside. Every year, fresh snow falls into these hollows. The weight of the snow eventually squeezes the air out of the bottom layers of the snow to form ice. Where this ice meets the rock below, pressure causes the ice to melt.

The melted water on the rock surface seeps into tiny cracks in the rock. At night, the water freezes and expands, forcing the cracks open. The next day, more water seeps in only to freeze again at night. Finally, a piece of rock breaks off. This process is called **freeze-thaw**.

In the hollow, the freeze-thaw causes more pieces of rock to break away, making the hollow bigger. The hollow is now called a **corrie**.

Moving ice

When the layer of ice becomes very heavy, it starts to flow out of the hollow and down the valley. It is now a glacier. As it moves downhill, the glacier picks up tonnes of broken rock, called **moraine**. This scrapes out the sides and floor of the valley.

Eventually, the glacier reaches the lowlands, where the air is warm enough for the ice to melt. The moraine is left behind, scattered over the lowland.

The long, narrow rivers of ice that flow down mountain valleys are called valley glaciers.

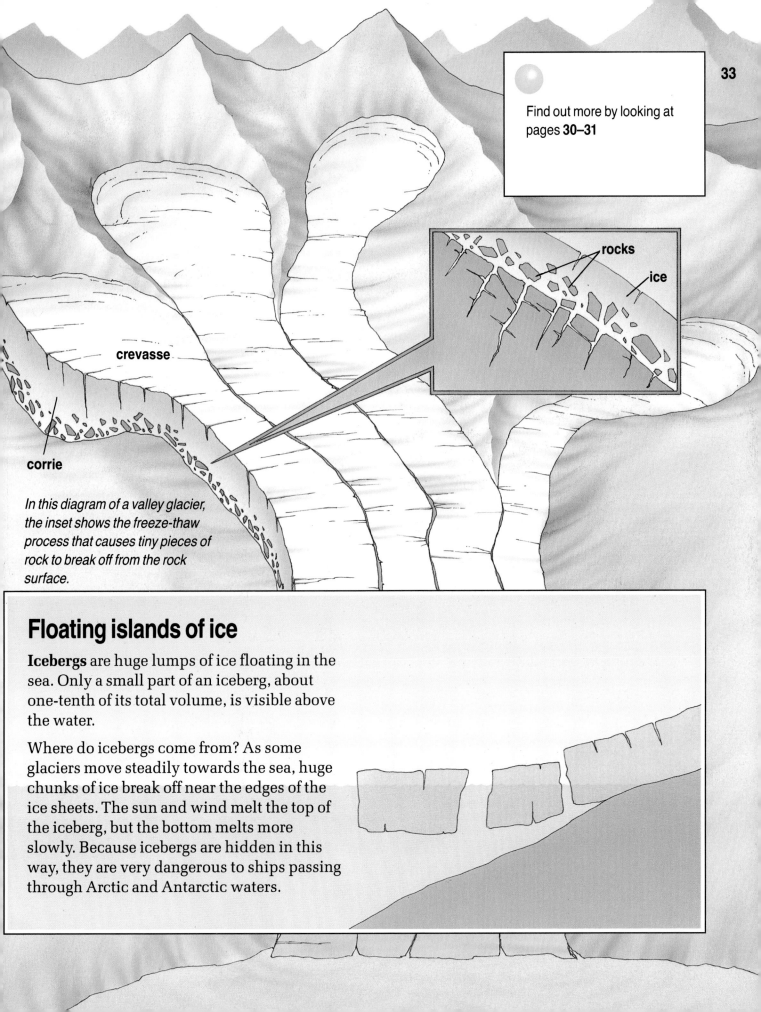

Find out more by looking at pages **30–31**

rocks

ice

crevasse

corrie

In this diagram of a valley glacier, the inset shows the freeze-thaw process that causes tiny pieces of rock to break off from the rock surface.

Floating islands of ice

Icebergs are huge lumps of ice floating in the sea. Only a small part of an iceberg, about one-tenth of its total volume, is visible above the water.

Where do icebergs come from? As some glaciers move steadily towards the sea, huge chunks of ice break off near the edges of the ice sheets. The sun and wind melt the top of the iceberg, but the bottom melts more slowly. Because icebergs are hidden in this way, they are very dangerous to ships passing through Arctic and Antarctic waters.

Days and seasons

A day lasts for 24 hours. But how do you know that a day has passed if you don't have a clock to measure the hours? In most places on Earth, you would see the sky darken and then become light again as the next day dawns. Do you know why?

A year lasts for about 365 days. But how do you know that a year has passed if you don't have a calendar to help you count the days? The amount of daylight varies at different times of the year. Let's find out how this happens.

The spinning Earth

Think of the Earth as an orange with a knitting needle stuck through the middle from the North Pole to the South Pole. This needle is like the axle that a wheel spins on. The Earth turns on this imaginary axle, or **axis**. Each complete turn, or revolution, takes 24 hours.

Daylight comes from the Sun. The parts of the spinning Earth that face the Sun are lit up. The parts of the Earth that face away from the Sun are in the dark.

How many seasons?

The Earth is not only turning on its axis, it is also moving around the Sun. It takes 365¼ days for our planet to circle the Sun, and we call this period of time, a year.

During the year, different parts of the Earth's surface face the Sun for longer or for shorter periods. In some parts of the world, these periods are known as the seasons. During the summer season, there is more daylight. In winter, there is less. In spring and autumn, the hours of light and dark are about the same. Some parts of the world only have two seasons. One may be rainy or dark, the other sunny or dry.

The Earth's axis is not at right angles to the Sun. It is slightly tilted. This means that each of the poles is tilted away from the Sun for half the year, and is therefore in the dark. For the other half of the year, each pole is tilted towards the Sun and is therefore bathed in sunlight, even at midnight. That's why the polar regions are called 'Lands of the Midnight Sun'.

The Earth takes one year to travel once around the Sun.

The Earth turns on its axis once every 24 hours.

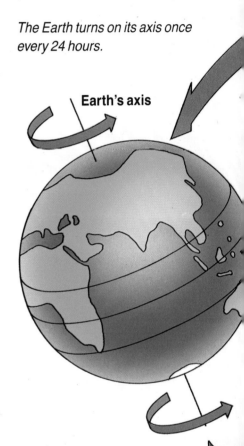

Earth's axis

In December, the South Pole is tilted towards the Sun. Places in the southern half of the Earth have more than 12 hours of daylight.

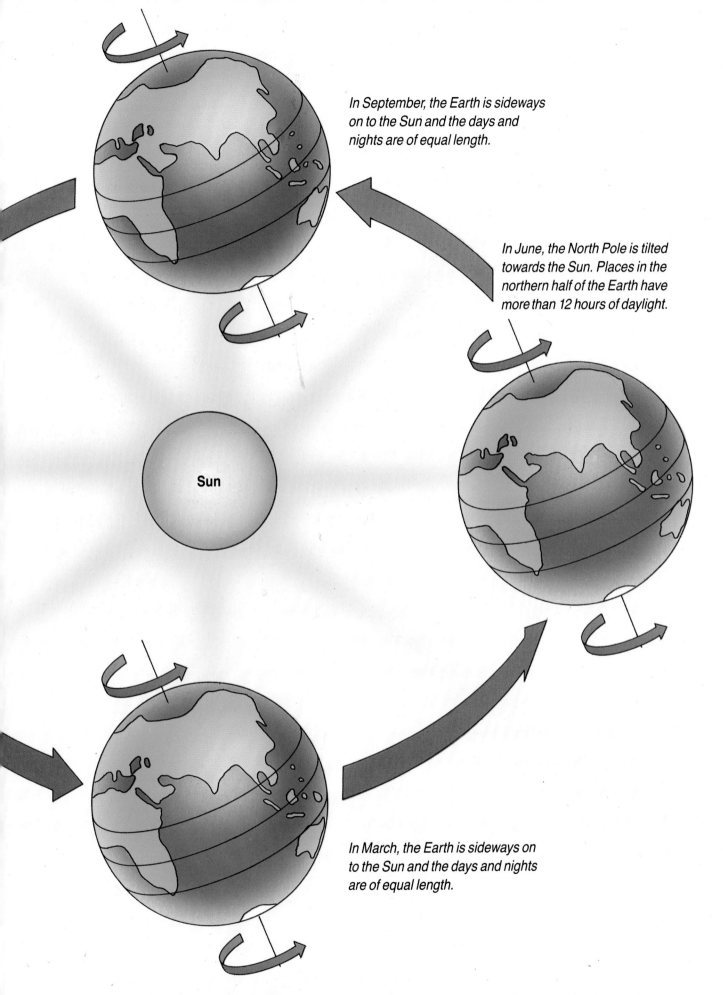

In September, the Earth is sideways on to the Sun and the days and nights are of equal length.

In June, the North Pole is tilted towards the Sun. Places in the northern half of the Earth have more than 12 hours of daylight.

In March, the Earth is sideways on to the Sun and the days and nights are of equal length.

Sun

Find out more by looking at pages **12–13**

What is the weather?

What is your weather like today? Is it sunny, cold, wet or dry? What causes these different kinds of weather? Heat and light from the Sun travel through the Earth's atmosphere. The Sun's rays affect the air in four ways. They can change its **temperature**, or the amount of heat it contains. They can change its **humidity**, or the amount of water it contains. They can change the **air pressure**, or the density of the air. And they can change the **wind**, or the way the air moves.

Temperature

Most of the heat given off by the Sun is lost in space. Then about one-third of the sunlight that does reach the atmosphere is reflected back into space by the clouds.

Less than half the sunlight that gets to the Earth's atmosphere actually reaches the planet's surface. This sunlight warms the ground, oceans and lakes, which then reflect warmth back into the air.

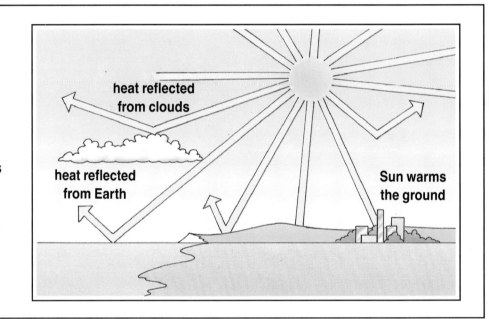

Humidity

Humidity is the amount of water vapour in the air. When sunlight warms oceans, lakes and rivers, some of the water turns into water vapour. The vapour rises into the air, condenses, and forms tiny drops of water that float in the air as clouds.

These drops fall to Earth as **precipitation**. That's what scientists call rain, snow, hail or sleet.

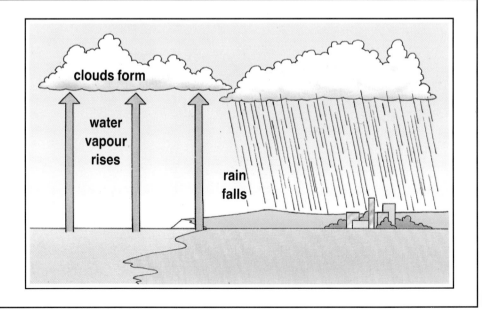

Air pressure

What difference does the weight of the air make? Warm air weighs less than cool air, which is why hot-air balloons stay up in the sky. Lighter weights put less pressure on whatever is underneath them.

So where there is warmer air, the air pressure is lower. Cool air weighs more, so where the air is cooler, the air pressure is higher.

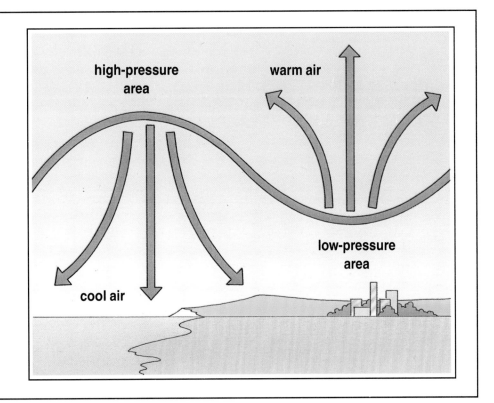

Wind

What is the wind? The wind is air moving from one place to another. Air always moves from where the pressure is high to where the pressure is low. The greater the difference between the levels of high pressure and low pressure, the stronger the wind movement.

Which way does the north wind blow? It blows from the north towards the south. Winds are always named after the direction from which they blow.

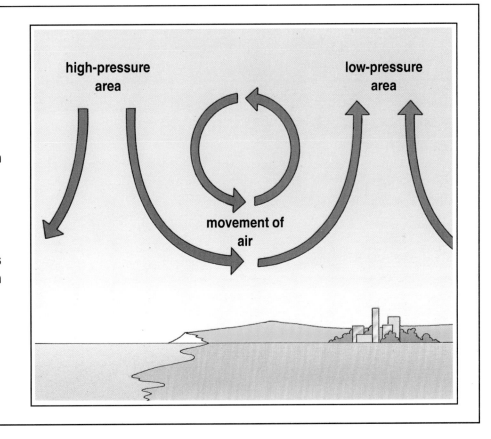

Find out more by looking at
pages **36–37**

Forecasting the weather

When you're planning a picnic with your friends, you need to know that the weather will be fine so that you can enjoy yourselves. Many people need to know what the weather will be like so that they can plan their work.

Scientists who study the weather are called **meteorologists**. They use many different instruments to collect information about temperature, air pressure, wind speed and direction. They also study the amount of moisture in the air.

You will need:

a pencil

a ruler

**a piece of thin card,
16 cm × 4 cm**

**a piece of stiff card,
24 cm × 30 cm**

a pair of scissors

sticky tape

**a strand of hair, about
25 cm long**

**a piece of wood, 24 cm × 4 cm
× 4 cm**

six drawing pins

a coloured pen with a fine point

How much moisture is there in the air?

You can make your own hygrometer. Keep a chart of your results every day for three weeks. Can you forecast whether it will be wet or dry during the fourth week?

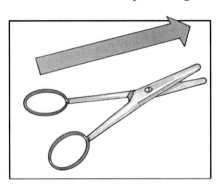

1. Using the ruler, draw an arrow about 13 centimetres by 2 centimetres on the thin card. Cut out the card arrow.

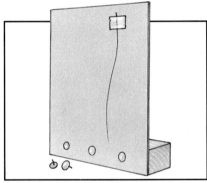

3. Using drawing pins, attach the stiff card to the long edge of the piece of wood.

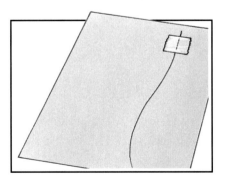

2. Stick one end of the strand of hair to the top of the stiff card.

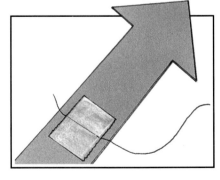

4. Attach the free end of the hair to the back of the arrow head.

Instruments for forecasting

Meteorologists measure the speed of the wind with a
radiosonde, and the amount of moisture with a **hygrometer**.
These instruments are used in weather stations on the
ground, or in aircraft, ships and weather balloons.
Meteorologists use the information from these instruments to
forecast what the weather is going to be like.

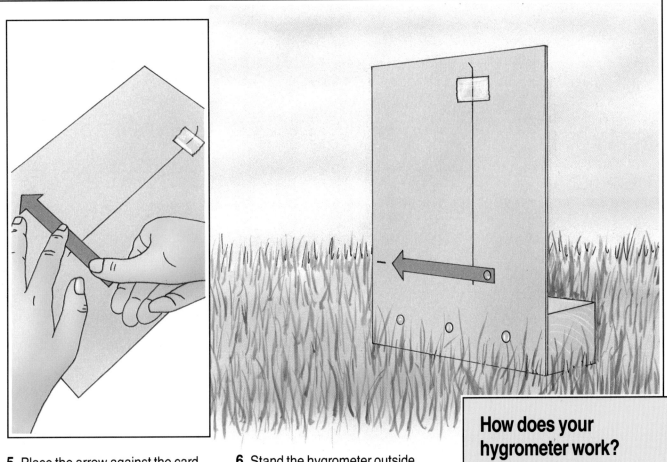

5. Place the arrow against the card
and move it until the hair is stretched
out fully. Then attach the other end
of the arrow to the card with a
drawing pin.

6. Stand the hygrometer outside.
Make sure that it can't fall over.
When the Sun is shining, mark on
the card where the arrow is pointing.
Write 'dry' by the side of this mark.
When the weather is damp, the
arrow will point lower. Mark its
new position and write 'damp'
on the card.

How does your hygrometer work?

On a damp day, the strand of
hair will absorb moisture from
the air. This will make the hair
stretch and so the arrow points
lower. On dry, sunny days the
hair dries out and becomes
shorter.

Find out more by looking at
pages **12–13**
      34–35
      36–37

What is a climate?

The weather near your home may be sunny one day and cloudy the next, or dry during one season and wet during another. Over several years, there's a pattern to these changes in the weather, wherever you live. This pattern is called a **climate**.

Scientists who study different climates are called **climatologists**. They say that the climate varies according to three things — the way the Sun's rays reach the Earth, the amount of land and sea nearby, and the height of the land above sea-level.

Climatologists divide the Earth into horizontal sections, using imaginary lines called **lines of latitude**. The line around the middle is called the **Equator**. The two main lines of latitude north of the Equator are called the Tropic of Cancer and the Arctic Circle. The two main lines of latitude south of the Equator are the Tropic of Capricorn and the Antarctic Circle.

The Sun's rays

Near the Equator, the Sun's rays shine from directly overhead. Here, the sunlight provides a lot of energy to heat up the land. In the polar regions, the Sun's rays meet the Earth's surface at a low angle. The sunlight is weaker here, because it is spread out over a wider area. It is also colder, because the rays have to pass through more of the Earth's atmosphere, and they lose heat on the way.

You can see that the Sun's rays are more concentrated at the Equator than anywhere else on Earth. So the countries near the Equator are the hottest in the world.

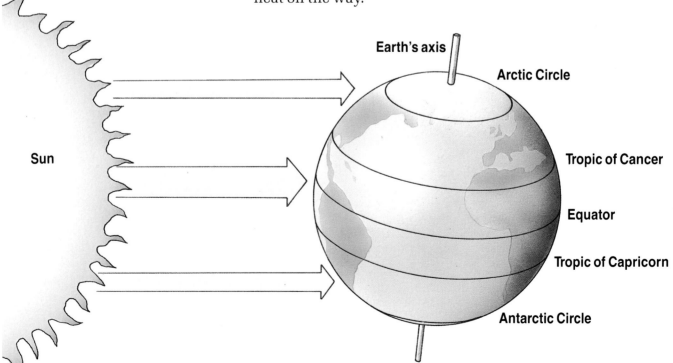

Earth's axis

Arctic Circle

Sun

Tropic of Cancer

Equator

Tropic of Capricorn

Antarctic Circle

What kind of climate?

Energy from the Sun warms the ground, and some of this heat is reflected back into the air. As the warm air rises, it cools down. Places that are high above sea-level, such as mountains, have cooler climates than places lower down.

Energy from the Sun warms the oceans, rivers and lakes, turning some of the water into vapour. This vapour rises to form clouds, and then falls back to Earth as rain, sleet, hail or snow. So places near the coast have wetter climates than places inland.

In tropical regions of the world, heavy rainfall often occurs during the hot seasons. In many countries, for example India, this heavy rain can cause flooding.

How the Sun shines

You will need:

a small ball

a torch

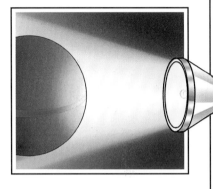

1. Hold the ball in one hand. Shine the torch beam directly onto the middle of the ball. The circle of bright light at the centre of the ball is similar to the Sun's rays shining at the Equator.

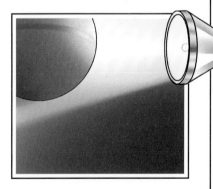

2. Now look at how the light is shining at the bottom of the ball. It is spread over a much wider area and is very dull right at the bottom. This shows how the Sun shines in the polar regions.

Stormy weather

Dark clouds fill the sky and heavy rain is pouring down. There are bright flashes of lightning and noisy thunder crashes. Do you know what causes these stormy sights and sounds?

What makes the clouds?

Heat from the Sun turns water from oceans and rivers into water vapour. Movements in the air, called **convection currents**, push the vapour up in the air. Here, it condenses and turns back into tiny drops of water.

The air is full of tiny particles of dust. A drop of water will collect around a dust particle. Clouds form where millions of these tiny drops of water gather. Thunderclouds are the biggest clouds of all. Some are as tall as 18 kilometres from top to bottom.

Lightning

During a storm, strong winds blow the tiny drops around dust particles inside the cloud and make them collide with one another. Normally, each particle in the cloud has what scientists call a positive and a negative electrical charge. But when the particles collide with each other, these charges separate. Most of the positive charges move to the top of the cloud and most of the negative charges move to the bottom.

Lightning is a giant spark of electricity in the sky. The spark happens when the negative charges in a thundercloud meet the positive charges in another cloud, or on the ground. Lightning strikes somewhere on the Earth about 100 times every second!

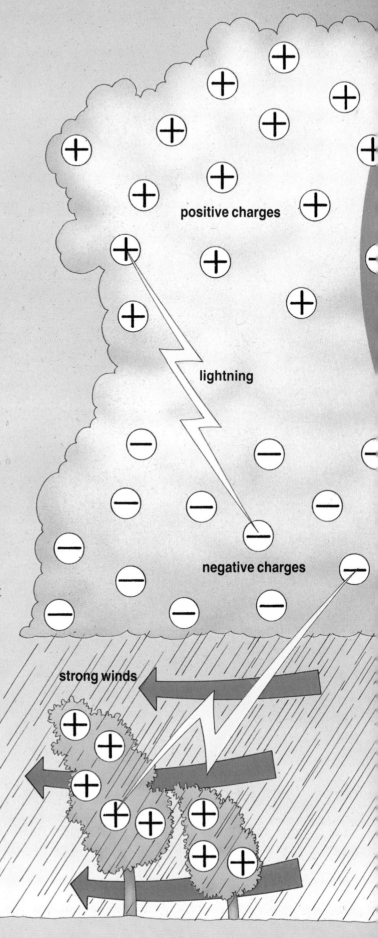

positive charges

lightning

negative charges

strong winds

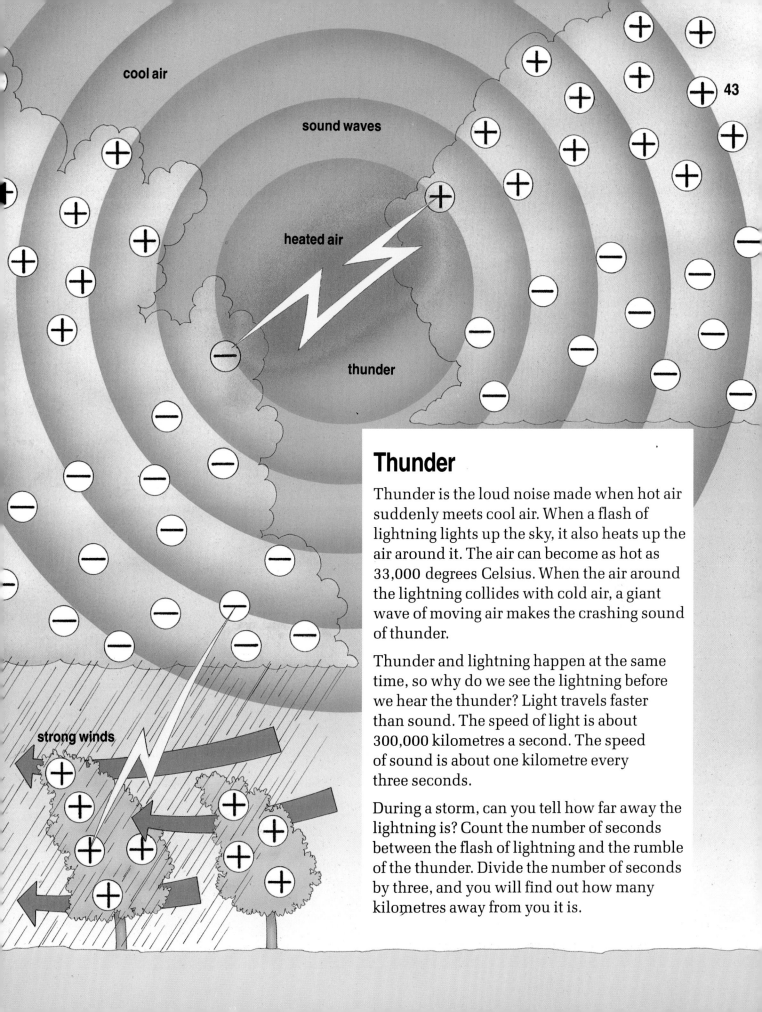

cool air

sound waves

heated air

thunder

strong winds

Thunder

Thunder is the loud noise made when hot air suddenly meets cool air. When a flash of lightning lights up the sky, it also heats up the air around it. The air can become as hot as 33,000 degrees Celsius. When the air around the lightning collides with cold air, a giant wave of moving air makes the crashing sound of thunder.

Thunder and lightning happen at the same time, so why do we see the lightning before we hear the thunder? Light travels faster than sound. The speed of light is about 300,000 kilometres a second. The speed of sound is about one kilometre every three seconds.

During a storm, can you tell how far away the lightning is? Count the number of seconds between the flash of lightning and the rumble of the thunder. Divide the number of seconds by three, and you will find out how many kilometres away from you it is.

Dangerous weather

The weather can sometimes be very dangerous. Violent storms can create fierce, twisting winds that seriously damage anything that gets in their way.

What is a tornado?

A **tornado** is a powerful, twisting wind storm. Most tornadoes develop along a boundary, called a **front**, where cool, dry air meets warm, humid air, and a black cloud forms in the sky.

If the warm air rises very quickly, more warm air rushes in to replace it. As this air rises, it sometimes starts to rotate. The rotating air forms a tornado, or twister, which is shaped like a long, thin funnel stretching down from the cloud towards the ground.

If this funnel meets the ground, it sucks things up like an enormous vacuum cleaner, making a swirling mass of dust and dirt. Tornadoes sometimes make houses explode! When the tornado sucks up air from around the outside of the house, it makes the air pressure outside lower than the air pressure inside. The force of the air inside pushes the walls apart and the house explodes!

In this tornado, the long, thin funnel of dust and dirt can be seen stretching from the clouds down to the ground.

The power of hurricanes

A **hurricane** is a powerful, whirling storm that starts over tropical oceans. Hurricanes can also be called typhoons, cyclones and willy-willies.

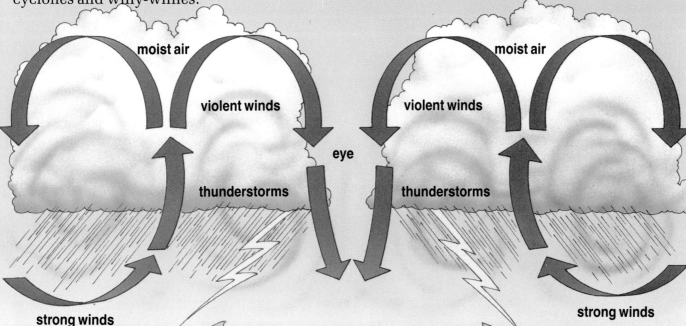

moist air

violent winds

eye

thunderstorms

moist air

violent winds

thunderstorms

strong winds

strong winds

In tropical regions, warm air rises quickly above the sea. It contains large amounts of water vapour that has evaporated from the sea below. Above the sea, the water vapour cools, turns back into water droplets and forms storm clouds. Sometimes, the very moist air travelling upwards meets strong winds that pull it up even higher. More moist air then rises from above the sea, making a huge, swirling ring of wind and rain.

Hurricane winds rotate at speeds of up to 240 kilometres an hour around a calm area in the centre, called the **eye** of the storm. The hurricane may last several days, moving forwards at about 20 kilometres an hour. Most of the damage caused by hurricanes happens because the storm creates huge waves that flood the land.

This kind of storm needs a constant supply of moist air rising from warm seas. So once they reach dry land, hurricanes die out.

If you could slice through a hurricane, this is how it would look. It consists of a huge mass of wind and rain, swirling at enormous speed around a still point in the middle, called the eye. A hurricane moves forwards as it rotates, creating huge, destructive waves in its path.

Water evaporates in the hot sun at these salt pans in Brazil. People can then collect the salt that is left behind.

Salt and the sea

Have you ever swum in the sea and accidentally swallowed some sea water? It probably made you cough and splutter. Sea water contains a lot of salt and this makes it very unpleasant to taste, as well as unhealthy to drink.

If you were to drink salt water, you would become thirsty. Do you know why? You already have lots of salt in your body — everybody has! If you take in even more, you would feel the need to drink some liquid to water down, or dilute, the extra salt.

We can make good use of both the water and the salt in the sea, but we need to separate them first.

Collecting salt

In some hot, dry countries people collect salt from the sea. Sea water is pumped into shallow ponds, called **salt pans**. The hot sunshine turns the water into vapour, or **evaporates** it, leaving behind salt crystals.

Human beings need to eat some salt to stay healthy. Animals also need salt, so farmers put out blocks of this important mineral for cattle to lick. Salt is mostly used to produce chemicals for manufacturing materials, such as glass, paper and plastics.

Making fresh water

People in some countries in the world are so short of fresh water that they are even thinking about towing icebergs from Arctic regions to their own dry lands! Ninety-seven per cent of the world's water is found in the oceans and seas.

Fresh water can be made by taking salt out of sea water. This process, called **desalination**, is expensive because it needs large amounts of energy, and the salt wears away the equipment. Saudi Arabia produces over 1,700 million litres of fresh water each day by desalination.

In the desalination process, the salt water is boiled and quickly turned into steam. The steam then condenses into fresh water.

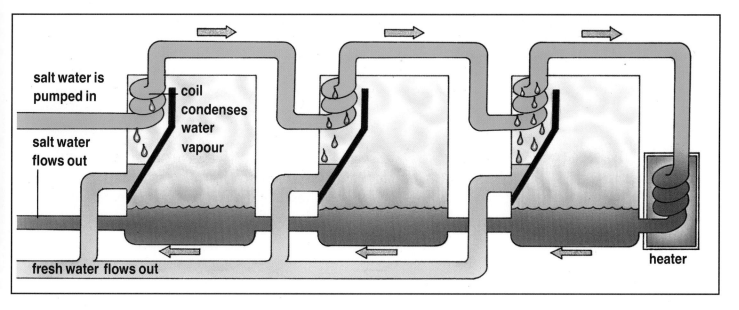

salt water is pumped in

coil condenses water vapour

salt water flows out

fresh water flows out

heater

Resources from the sea

Have you ever tasted sea water? It tastes quite salty. As rivers flow over rocks towards the sea, many other useful minerals, called **salts**, dissolve in the water. In this way, millions of tonnes of **gold salts** and **silver salts** have been dissolved in the sea. Every natural element can be found in the waters of the ocean.

Much of the world's supply of **magnesium** is taken out, or extracted, directly from sea water. Magnesium is mixed with aluminium to make light metals. **Bromine** is also extracted from sea water and used to manufacture medicines, as well as photographic film.

Food from the sea

The sea provides us with food. Every year, 77 million tonnes of fish and shellfish are taken from the sea. Some kinds of algae, such as dulses, are also good to eat. Other algae provide chemicals, called **alginates**, that are used to make sausages and paper.

These fishermen are pulling the nets back on board their fishing boat. Many large fishing boats also carry equipment to sort out the catch of fish.

Mining the sea-bed

Deep down on the sea-bed, there are fist-sized lumps, or **nodules**, that contain lots of minerals. The nodules are made up of layers, like an onion. They are found in areas where many sea creatures live. The sea creatures collect and store minerals in their bodies. When they die and sink to the bottom of the sea, the minerals in their bodies are left in the mud.

These nodules usually contain **iron** and **manganese**, which are used to make hard steel for tools. Some nodules contain valuable minerals like **cobalt**, **nickel** and **copper**.

The special machines that mine the nodules on the sea-bed operate by remote control. They suck up the nodules from the sea-bed like huge vacuum cleaners.

It is more difficult and expensive to extract minerals from the sea than from the ground. But the reserves of minerals on land are quickly being used up. So we need to use the sea's resources.

Special machines are used to collect minerals from the sea-bed. This hydraulic mining system is a prototype used for lifting manganese ore to the surface.

Resources from the Earth's crust

Everything on Earth is made up of a combination of building blocks called the **chemical elements**. There are 85 different elements in nature, and most of these are metals. Most metals can combine with other chemical elements to form **compounds**. These compounds are called minerals when they are found in rocks and soil.

How do metals form?

Minerals may form where molten rocks from beneath the Earth's crust cool and harden. These metal-containing rocks are called **ores**. The large iron ore deposits in Kiruna, in northern Sweden, were formed in this way.

As the molten rocks cool, a mixture of minerals, gas and hot water forces its way into cracks in the rocks. Here it cools and hardens to form thin lines that are rich in metallic minerals like **lead**, **copper** and **zinc**.

Some metal elements do not combine easily with other elements. These metals, like **gold**, **silver** and **platinum**, occur naturally in the Earth's crust as small grains, or as larger lumps of metal. Falling rain and rivers wash these metals out of rocks on the Earth's surface. The heavier metals collect in one area and form **placer deposits**.

When these deposits occur on river beds, special dredgers sort the metals from gravel deposits. Powerful water jets are used to break up dry placer deposits. The gravel is washed and separated from the metal ore. Another way of finding metal ores is to dig them out of the ground. This is called mining. Mining for different metals is carried out in many parts of the world.

The layer of iron ore is clearly visible in this rock from an open-cast iron ore mine.

This enormous, open-cast, iron ore mine is situated at Mount Whaleback in Western Australia.

Special machines are used to drill into the rock surfaces in underground iron ore mines.

Mining

Mining for metals can take place on the Earth's surface or underground. Surface mining is called **open-cast mining**. First, diggers remove the soil and rocks above the ore. If the ore is hard, it is broken up with the help of explosives.

To mine ores that are buried deep underground, miners have to cut a vertical shaft with horizontal tunnels into the rock. They may use explosives to blast free the ore, before removing it. This is a dangerous and expensive method of mining metals. Or sometimes powerful machines cut slices of ore from the rock face and load them on to trucks. These are then taken up to the surface.

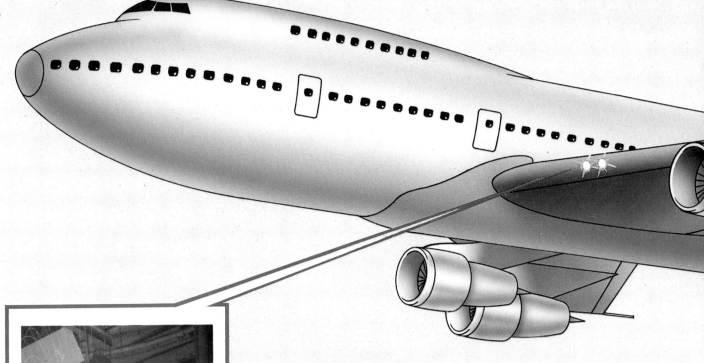

Copper is found in several different kinds of ore. The rock is removed from the ore and the remaining material passes through a smelter, which removes the copper.

All about metals

Do you know how many different metals are used to build an aeroplane? There are three main metals. **Aluminium** is needed to make the body of the aeroplane. A special, strong metal called **titanium** is used to build parts of the aeroplane's engines. Hundreds of metres of **copper** wire connect all the electrical parts of the aeroplane.

Where do these different metals come from? They are all found in the Earth's crust, either as pieces of pure metal or as the minerals that make up ores. Metals can be mixed together to make a new substance called an **alloy**.

Metals for different jobs

Metals that are used to make bridges, railway lines and buildings need to be hard and strong, like **steel**. Some metals are hard and strong but they snap easily. These metals are brittle. **Iron** is an example of a brittle metal.

It is easy to work with other metals, like **gold**, because you can hammer or roll them into shapes, or stretch them and they won't break. Magnetic metals, like **iron**, are useful because they can attract or repel magnets. Some metals, like **sodium**, are soft and others, like **mercury**, are liquid.

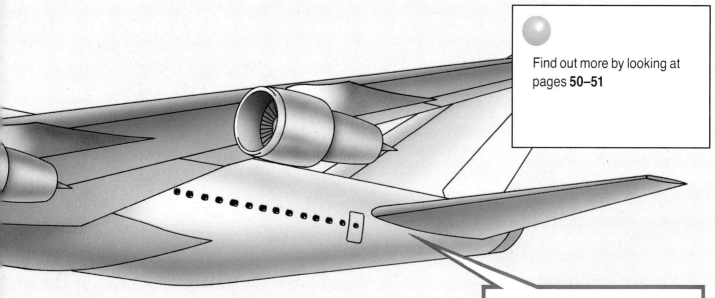

Find out more by looking at pages **50–51**

Tin comes from the ore **cassiterite**. It is easy to bend but it is difficult to corrode or wear away. Tin is used to join, or solder, metals together. Some cans are made from steel with a thin coating of tin to stop them from becoming rusty. Cans containing soft drinks are made of lightweight aluminium, which comes from an ore called **bauxite**.

Precious metals

We sometimes call valuable metals, such as platinum and gold, precious metals. **Platinum** is the most valuable metal in the world. It is called a **catalyst** because it produces a chemical reaction in other substances without itself changing. Platinum is more expensive than gold and is used in many industries.

Gold is the third most valuable metal after platinum and **iridium**. It can be rolled and stretched more than any other metal. Gold is used to make jewellery and some electronic equipment. Copper is often added to gold to make it harder.

Another precious metal is **silver**, which loses its shine, or lustre, when exposed to the air. Silver must be polished to remove any stains. The photographic film in your camera contains silver, and many ornaments and pieces of jewellery are made of silver.

Aluminium can be flattened between rollers to make sheets of metal. Aluminium sheeting is used on buildings, in machinery and in trains, and ships.

Gemstones

When molten rock from beneath the Earth's surface cools, the minerals inside it may form into crystals. These have many different shapes, different numbers of sides and sharp corners. Some of these crystals are called **gemstones**. They are also known as **gems**.

Gems are very hard. They are sometimes washed into rivers because the surrounding rock where they have formed has worn away. **Diamonds** are the hardest of all known minerals. They formed from carbon millions of years ago. The carbon, surrounded by hot volcanic rock, cooled very slowly and became diamond.

Many different industries use diamonds because of the hardness of these gems. Diamonds can cut through hard metals quickly and accurately. They are also used in mining and drilling. Did you know there is a diamond in the needle of most record players?

You will need:

string

a teaspoon

hot water

a paperclip

a pencil

washing soda crystals

two glass jars

a small bowl

Grow your own crystals

You can grow some crystals for yourself by adding washing soda to a jar of hot water. After a few days in a warm room, the crystals will begin to grow.

1. Put the teaspoon into the jar and fill up the jar with hot water.

Danger: Hot water can scald!

2. Add a few teaspoons of washing soda to the water and stir the mixture. Add some more washing soda and stir the mixture again.

Lasers

Rubies and **sapphires** come from a mineral called corundum. Tiny quantities of chromium in the mineral give it the red colour of rubies. In industry, rubies are used to produce lasers. The ruby crystal helps to produce a strong, thin beam of light that can cut and melt with great accuracy. Lasers are used in industry, in medicine, in communications and in scientific research.

Diamonds are so hard that one diamond is needed to cut another one. A rough diamond like this can have as many as 58 sides after it has been cut and polished.

3. Fill the bowl with hot water and stand the jar in it. Keep on adding more soda to the jar and keep stirring until the soda stops dissolving in the water. Allow the liquid to cool and pour it into the second jar.

4. Tie a paperclip to one end of the string. Tie the other end around the pencil. Place the pencil across the top of the jar so that the paperclip hangs in the water. After a few days you will have a large lump of crystals.

Survey of materials

There are so many different things in the world around us. Some are natural and some are artificial, some were once alive and others never have been. There are solids and liquids and gases. But everything you look at must have come from either the land, the sea or the air. These three parts of the world provide us with all the different materials we need.

Before we can use materials, we have to sort them out. This helps us to choose the right material with the right qualities, or **properties**, for our purpose. If we make something from the wrong materials, it just won't work properly. Imagine what this book would be like made from sheets of steel rather than from sheets of paper!

A good way to sort out materials is to look at their properties. This means seeing what a material does when you test it. Simple tests include heating, bending, hammering, scratching and putting in water.

Do some simple tests

You will need:

some samples, such as wood, salt, pebbles, a tin lid, aluminium foil

an old dish

an oven

a hammer

a bowl of water

1. Try bending a larger sample with your hands.

2. Place a very small sample on an old dish and place it in a cold oven. Heat up the oven, then switch it off and wait until it is cool before removing the sample.

Testing different materials

Try collecting 20 or more materials from in and around your home. It is best to start with simple materials, like a piece of wood, a spoonful of salt or a pebble. Try not to collect things that are made from more than one material.

The survey sheet shown below will help you to sort out your collection and to discover the properties of each material. Some materials have already been written down on the sheet to show you how to do it. Draw up your own survey sheet using these ideas as a starting point. With practice, you can invent your own tests to suit the types of material in your collection.

Make sure you ask an adult to check your tests are safe and to help you with your activities.

When you have tested your material, fill in the result on your survey sheet. Your list of results will help you to find out the different properties of the material.

3. Wrap each sample in a cloth and hit it with a hammer. Does it shatter?

4. Leave each sample in a bowl of water. Does it float or sink? Does it change if you leave it there for a few days?

	Material	Heating	Bending	Hammering	Add water	Natural or artificial or both?	Metallic or non-metallic or both?
1.	Wood	burns	splinters	dents	floats	natural	non-metallic
2.	Salt	nothing	—	powders	dissolves	natural	metallic
3.	pebbles						
4.	tin lid						
5.	aluminium foil						
6.							
7.							
8.							

Find out more by looking at
pages **48–49**
50–51

Resources from our planet

Everything we use each day comes from either the land, the sea or the air. Metals are extracted from ores dug out of the ground. Some medicines contain chemicals found in sea water. Crops are grown with the help of fertilizers that contain nitrogen from the atmosphere, and hydrogen from natural gas. Electricity is generated from the energy in coal. Cars and lorries run on fuel made from crude oil. Coal, oil and natural gas are all fossil fuels that are found beneath the Earth's surface.

All the materials that we take out of the ground, the sea or the air are called **resources**. We are steadily using them up.

Coal is a fossil fuel that is used mainly to produce electricity. The Earth has only a limited supply of fossil fuels and we will eventually use them all up.

Renewable resources, like trees, can be replaced. They will never run out if we keep planting new ones.

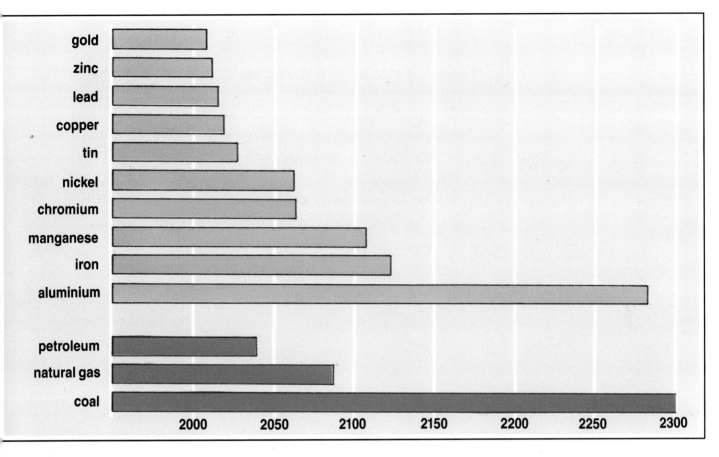

Non-renewable and renewable resources

There is a vast amount of air in the atmosphere — about 5,000 million million tonnes! There is even more water in the seas. We may never use up all the resources in the air and in the seas. But there is a danger that we may pollute them and therefore make them useless.

Resources such as metal ores, coal, oil and natural gas formed in the ground millions of years ago. As we use them, they are not being replaced, or renewed. We say that these resources are **non-renewable**.

Other resources are **renewable**, which means they can be replaced. We can generate small amounts of electricity from the power of the wind or the waves. Hot rocks deep inside the Earth's crust can be used to boil water to make steam. This steam can turn a turbine and generate electricity. We can keep growing trees and other plants and use them to make paper and wood products, fuels and chemicals.

This chart shows how long the world's resources of certain minerals and fossil fuels will last, if we continue to use them as fast as we are doing today and if new deposits are not discovered.